Spotlight on
Motor rac

Roger Price

GW01464147

Cassell Graded Readers Level 3

General Editor: Michael Carrier

Cassell
London

CASSELL LTD
35 Red Lion Square, London WC1R 4SG
an affiliate of
Macmillan Publishing Co Inc
New York

First published 1982

British Library Cataloguing in Publication Data

Price, Roger
    Spotlight on motor racing. — (Cassell graded
    readers; level 3)
    1. English language — Textbooks for foreigners
    2. Readers — Automobile racing
    I. Title
    428.6'4   PE1128

ISBN 0-304-30565-0

Printed in Hong Kong by Wing King Tong Printing Co. Ltd.

Our thanks are due to the following for permission
to reproduce photographs:

National Motor Museum (pp 8, 19, 23, 37, 40, 47)
British Tourist Authority (p 10)
Ford (pp 12, 14, 26)
Aerofilms (pp 30, 31)
Autocar (p 43)

Contents

Preface

This is a new series of readers for foreign students of English. It is new in several ways. Firstly, it has been designed as a series rather than an arbitrary group of titles. Secondly, the series provides reading material that is representative of the students' interests and corresponds as far as possible to the books that students would read in their own language. Thus it consists only of informative, entertaining, non-fiction topics. Thirdly, the language used in the readers has been carefully chosen and controlled so as to be easily understandable for students without being childish or patronising in its tone. At the same time each reader introduces a sizeable amount of subject-specific vocabulary which would not normally be included in a simple grading system. This subject-specific vocabulary is carefully explained through text, illustration or glossary so that the student can deal with topics in a more serious and informative way.

There are six levels, Level 1 being the simplest and Level 6 the most difficult. Each level introduces *circa* 350 new headwords and the length of each reader depends on its level (cf. list of titles at the beginning of this book).

The language is controlled lexically according to a

grading system, and subject-specific vocabulary is added where appropriate. There is also a structural grading which keeps syntactic complexity to a level that is comprehensible to the student. This operates mainly in Levels 1-4.

As one of the main aims of Cassell's Graded Readers is to stimulate the students' interest and motivation to read, the books are presented in a lively and interesting format and are well illustrated throughout. Each book also contains follow-up exercises and activities to give students the opportunity to take their interest in the topic, as well as in the language, further than a merely passive reading of the text.

Further details of the linguistic grading can be found in the Teachers' Guide to the series, obtainable from the publishers.

Colchester, 1982   Michael Carrier
                                         General Editor

1
Motor racing then and now

The first races

In 1885 Carl-Friedrich Benz built the very first car with a petrol engine. Only ten years later the first important motor race took place, from Paris to Bordeaux and back again, a distance of 1178 kilometres. Not many cars were able to finish the race: some of them broke down*, others crashed*. Some of the drivers became so tired that they stopped their cars and fell asleep.

The first car which reached Paris was a Panhard-Levassor. Emile Levassor built the car with his friend René Panhard. Levassor drove it in the race. He wore a thick coat, gloves* and a bowler hat*. The car had no roof, an engine with only one cylinder*, wooden wheels with solid* rubber* tyres and oil lamps. It could travel at about 60 kilometres an hour.

For the next few years Levassor, Panhard and other car builders, most of them French, went on building racing cars. They tested the cars in motor races all over Europe.

These races became faster and faster, and more and more dangerous. The people who were watching, the spectators, did not understand that fast cars were such a danger to them. They used to walk on the roads while the cars were going past and the children used to play a game

---

* See *Glossary*.
  New words are asterisked (*) the first time they occur only.

One of the first motor races: Paris-Madrid 1903

with the cars to see how brave they were. The last one who crossed the road before a racing car went past was the winner. In the race from Paris to Madrid in 1903, cars travelled at 100 kilometres an hour, or even faster. Their brakes* were very bad, the roads were awful and there were a lot of accidents*. Drivers drove into trees and knocked down spectators. Several people died and a lot were badly hurt. The organisers* stopped the race, and soon after this all the governments in Europe stopped motor racing on public roads.

The first Grand Prix Race (*Grand Prix* is French for *Big Prize**) took place in 1906 at Le Mans, not far from Paris. There the organisers built a special circuit (a road only for motor racing) which was about 100 kilometres long. The cars had to go round the circuit six times on the first day of the race and six times on the second day. The weather was very hot and the road very bad. Every driver had problems with the car tyres: they became very hot and either went flat or broke into small pieces. The organisers did not let anyone help the driver and his mechanic* when they had to change tyres.

Racing today

Since those first races, many things have changed in motor racing. It is no longer the world of the hobby mechanic* and the part-time driver. Motor racing is now big business, not only for the car builders and drivers, but also for large industrial companies* who put a lot of money into the sport.

Look at today's Grand Prix driver. He is much busier than the driver of 70 years ago. He travels much more from one country to another, from one race to another. He practises a lot more with his car to make it better, safer and faster. If a driver wins a lot of races he can become as famous and as rich as a pop singer or a film star. He can take part in television and radio programmes, he can write in newspapers and magazines, and he can even help to sell cars, petrol or cigarettes.

The life of a Grand Prix racing driver today is also a much more dangerous one, so the driver must always think about safety in motor racing. He knows, for example, that if a car crashes in a race it can easily catch fire* and the driver can easily burn to death*. For that reason he must wear clothes made of special material

The driver must always think about safety

which will not burn in an accident. His car must also carry
automatic fire extinguishers*.

Sometimes the racing driver of today thinks more
about safety than the race organisers. A few years ago, for
example, many drivers were not willing to race on the
famous Nurburgring racing circuit in West Germany. It
was to dangerous for a Grand Prix race because there were
too many bends — the places where the road turns. There
were also too many hills and too many trees near the road.
The drivers have a very powerful voice, so, in the end, the
Grand Prix organisers decided to hold the race on another
circuit.

Look now at today's racing car. In the early days of
motor racing there were cars with steam*, electric and
petrol engines in the same race. This is not possible

today. There are now many different sorts of racing and each has its own list of rules* (which we call a formula). The most important rules are for the size of the car and the amount* of petrol which the car can carry. The rules also say how long each sort of race must be.

All these rules are in a thick pocket book called the *Yellow Book*. When a car builder wants to make a car for Grand Prix racing he looks at the rules which make Formula number 1. The size of the Formula 1 engine must be 3000 cubic centimetres and it must have not more than twelve cylinders. The car must not weigh less than 575 kilograms and must not be wider than 140 centimetres. So the builder of a Formula 1 car must follow these rules and at the same time try to make his car better and faster than the other builders.

The rules do not say what the shape of the car must be — and there is no perfect shape for a Grand Prix car. One shape is better when the car travels fast, another shape is better when the car goes round bends. So the car builder must decide which is the best shape for both the bends and the straight parts of a circuit.

In the end the driver is the most important part of the car. If his car is as fast as the others in a race and if he is the best driver in the race, then he should come first. The problem is that anything can happen in a race. . .

In this book we will spend most of the time in the world of Formula 1 racing, but we must not forget the other sorts of racing which can be just as exciting and dangerous.

Formula 2 or Formula 3 races, for example, take place

A Formula 1 car

all over the world. Many of the Grand Prix stars of the future learn their difficult job at the steering-wheel* of Formula 2 and 3 cars which are less powerful and expensive than Formula 1 cars. There are other formulas for those who want to race with sports cars or 'normal' saloon cars (which are closed, not like open sports cars) such as Ford Escorts or Volkswagens. In Britain there are even formulas for races with cars which are almost as old as motor racing itself. These are vintage cars — very old cars. The Vintage Sports Car Club organises regular race meetings for cars which started racing before 1914. Some vintage car drivers say that their races can be just as dangerous as Grand Prix races not only because the cars are so tall, big and heavy, but also because some of them can travel at over 160 kilometres an hour!

Whatever the car, motor racing is becoming more and more popular* all over the world. Even young children want to go racing — in 'go-karts'. These are very small racing-cars with wheels only a few centimetres high and with engines which you usually find in lawn-mowers*.

James Hunt

2
The story of a racing driver

The start

James Hunt has always been a good sportsman. When he was at school near London he played squash* and tennis*. He was also a very good cross country runner. His father wanted him to study medicine, and James himself was quite willing to become a doctor.

On his 18th birthday James went to a motor racing meeting with a few friends. While he was watching the cars race round the racing circuit at Silverstone he suddenly decided that he wanted to become a world champion* racing driver.

Becoming champion driver of the world is not the easiest thing to do. James had to start his racing career* somewhere. For a short time he sold ice cream, then drove a lorry, then worked in a hospital, then in a supermarket. In the end he saved enough money to buy a secondhand* Mini. He worked on the car for two years before he could race with it. When the car was ready he took it to the Snetterton racing circuit for his very first race. But when he arrived, the organisers took one look at his car and decided he could not take part* because the Mini had neither a windscreen* nor side windows.

James raced for a few months with his Mini in some

other races and then bought a 'real' racing car, an Alexis. In his first race he finished 'about fifth' and in his next race he was second. A year later he bought a secondhand* Formula 3 racing car and was now closer to Grand Prix racing and the world championship than ever before. He raced about half a dozen* times. He drove very well in all the races — so well that he received a special prize. He bought a newer and bigger car and travelled all over Europe, from one Formula 3 race to another.

It was a difficult life. He lived in a tent* for most of the time in order to save money. He earned just enough money in his races to eat, travel and pay for new parts for his car. He won his first international race in Rouen, France. Then the problems began. He had several small crashes and one big one in Holland where his car, a March, turned upside down. In other races his car gave him a lot of trouble and he was not able to finish. In the end he decided to leave the March team, where he worked for over a year. James wanted to race alone.

James and a lord

Lord Hesketh, a rich young lord*, had a new hobby — motor racing. He was looking for a fast young driver to join his racing team. When he knew that James Hunt was no longer with the March team, he offered him a place in his team. James accepted*.

A short time later, James drove in an important Formula 2 race in Britain and came third. He did well in other races in Europe — and Lord Hesketh decided it was time to enter* Formula 1 racing — where the best driver becomes world champion.

The team needed a long time to get a car ready for the first Formula 1 race. The car which they had was good, but secondhand. When the time came for the race, James still needed to practise a lot. But he drove the powerful car well and finished third.

James Hunt took part in a Grand Prix race for the first time in Monaco. Newspaper reporters followed the young newcomer* everywhere before and after the race. Lord Hesketh was very popular with the photographers who took photos of his yacht*, helicopter* and Rolls Royce, as well as photos of the pretty young ladies who were with the racing team! In the race itself James drove very well on the difficult circuit. Towards the end of the race he was in sixth place, but then something went wrong with his engine and he had to stop racing.

For the next two years James did quite well in Grand Prix racing, but never came first.* When he won for the first time — in the Dutch Grand Prix — he drove a car which the Hesketh team built themselves. It seemed, at last, that James Hunt's dream of the world championship could come true.

A new team and new problems

James was becoming a better driver, but the racing was costing the Hesketh team more and more money. The team really needed somebody to help pay all the costs. But Lord Hesketh did not want anybody from outside in his team. This meant that the Hesketh team could not continue racing. So James Hunt had to look for another team.

He was lucky*. McLaren – Marlboro, a good team with good mechanics and good cars, offered James a place. But his first year with the team was full of problems, dangers and difficulties. In the American Grand Prix another driver pushed James off the racing circuit and his car drove into a wall. In the Spanish Grand Prix James came first, but the organisers who measured his car after the race found that it was 1.8 centimetres too wide. So they gave the first place, the first prize and the highest number of championship points* to the driver who came second — Niki Lauda. In the Belgian and Monaco Grand Prix races Hunt's car broke down.

By this time James was 47 championship points behind the leader, Niki Lauda. But James was still fighting! He won the French Grand Prix, and won back the first place in the championship (which he had lost in the Spanish Grand Prix.) The organisers decided that James' car was too wide but that he could keep his first place and the championship points. Then, in front of thousands of his fans*, James won the British Grand Prix. But after the race he had more problems with the race organisers. They decided that his win did not count because he stopped his car at the beginning of the race when there was a crash.

In the next Grand Prix, at the Nurburgring in West Germany. Niki Lauda crashed, his car caught fire* and he was badly burnt. James won the race, and he now had 44 championship points. Lauda was in hospital, but he was

Monaco Grand Prix

still the leader with 58 points. But when he returned to the Grand Prix fight he was only two points in front of Hunt. In his next race Lauda finished fourth but Hunt skidded* off the circuit and stopped racing. There were now only three more races before the end of the season. Hunt won the first two, but was still behind Lauda on points. The last Grand Prix in Japan was the most important of his whole life.

Niki Lauda

Fight to the finish

It was dark and it was raining heavily when the race started. James was the leader at the start. Niki Lauda was at the back and was falling behind*. After two laps Lauda stopped: he could not see well because of the recent* operation* on his eyes and because of the heavy rain. It seemed that Hunt was going to win.

Then the rain stopped and Hunt had problems with one of his tyres: it was slowly losing air. Should he continue to race and hope that the tyre did not go flat, or should he change the tyre? It was difficult to tell which was best. Hunt stopped, and the mechanics changed all the wheels on his car in 27 seconds! Hunt could drive faster now — and faster than the others because his car now had tyres for dry weather. The other cars still had rain tyres on their wheels.

But, because of the stop, Hunt was now in sixth place. He had to finish fourth or better to win the world championship. He drove faster than ever before. He passed the car in fifth position*, then the one in fourth . . . and the race was over.

As he left the circuit, thousands of people cheered the new world champion.

3
The men behind the man behind the wheel

The team

The race is over, the crowds cheer and the winner of the Grand Prix race waves to them. Later, there is a lot of champagne*, the cameras flash* and everyone shakes the hand of the smiling winner. It is very easy to forget at that moment that it is not only the driver who has won, but also a large team of people who have helped in many ways before and during* the race.

We have already seen a little of what the mechanics do. Usually two of them look after* each car in a race. Before the start they look carefully at the car and engine to check that all is well. When the race is on they wait in a special place at the side of the racing circuit called a pit. When the driver has a problem with his car he drives to the pit where the mechanics can do repairs very quickly. Sometimes the driver decides to put different tyres on his car because the weather has changed. The mechanics can do this for him very quickly. In a long distance race (not a Grand Prix race) the driver will have to stop and fill up with petrol. Good mechanics, who have practised very hard, can fill up a car in less than half a minute with special petrol pumps*.

The mechanics are not the only people in the pits.

Grand Prix cars usually belong to teams and each team usually enters two cars for each Grand Prix. At least eleven people work for the team. There is the team manager (the boss) who organises everything and makes plans for the future. He has an assistant to help him and a secretary to write letters for him. You can often see one of

A car in the pits at Indianpolis Speedway, USA

them with a stopwatch* which can measure .01 seconds, and the other with a special notice board for the team drivers. This board tells the drivers their exact places in the race.

Although only two cars take part in the race, the team keeps a third car to replace* one of the others if it breaks down before the race. So the team will have six mechanics, two for each car. There are two other very important people: one who looks after the spare* parts for the cars and another who makes those parts for the cars which the team cannot buy.

This team — and the cars — travel all over the world to the different race meetings. When there is a race, perhaps in Brazil, racing cars from Europe go either by plane or by ship. Flying is fast, but very expensive. The journey by ship is cheaper, but can take a couple* of weeks. When the race is much nearer home, the cars — and spare* parts — travel in a large lorry called a transporter. So the driver of the transporter becomes a new and very important member of the team.

The cost

About one dozen* racing teams take part in the Formula 1 World Championship. Each team must spend about half a million pounds (£500,000) a year to race two cars. Top* drivers, who have shown that they can win Grand Prix races, receive a good share* of the money. Some of the money goes towards the wages* of the team members, some goes towards travel costs. But the team needs most of the money for the cars.

Building the car body and buying the engine for it costs a lot of money. When the first car is ready it will cost more than a Rolls Royce. But the second and third cars cost much less because they are only copies of the first. Each car needs two engines — one for practice and one for the race, and each engine can cost over £20,000. The wide wheels on today's racing cars are very expensive. Although the tyres for the wheels do not cost much, the team will probably use over two hundred in one year.

When the race is over, the team must send the engines of each car back to the makers. They make a very careful check* of all the parts. They then put the engine back together and send it back to the team (together with a large bill!)

Where does the money come from to pay these bills? Some, but not all, comes from the prize money which the organisers of a race give to the successful* teams. The winner will receive about £5,000 for first place, and even those who finish near the bottom will receive some money. But is clear that even when the same team wins every Grand Prix race in one year, the prize money will not be enough to pay the costs of racing two cars.

This is where we meet more men behind the man behind the wheel.

Who pays: the sponsors

The sponsors play a very important part in motor racing. As soon as you look at a Grand Prix car you can see how important they are. Stickers* on the cars shout out the names of petrol companies, tyre companies, camera-makers and perfume*-makers. These are the sponsors — the people who give money to Grand Prix teams to help them pay the heavy costs of Formula 1 motor racing.

The sponsors hope that a lot of people will see their stickers not only at the racing circuit but also on the television sports news and in newspaper photos. They hope also that people will remember the names on these stickers when they go to buy petrol, tyres, perfume or a camera.

Tyre companies are often the most important sponsors. They supply all the tyres which a team needs, usually with their name in large letters on the side of the tyre. Oil com-

James Hunt in a car sponsored by Texaco and Marlboro

panies are also important because they supply the special petrol which the cars need for racing. Some companies offer so much help and money that they want their name to be part of the name of the team or car. So, in past Grand Prix races, cars and teams with names such as Yardley – McLaren and Elf – Tyrell have taken part. The first part of the name is the name of the team sponsor, the second part of the name is that of the car maker.

Cigarette makers have begun to take a great interest in motor racing. They have had to find other ways to show the public the names of their cigarettes because they can no longer do this on most television stations in the world. Motor racing is a fast sport which is popular all over the world. So now, when people go to watch a race or see a film of it on television, they can see cigarette names everywhere — on the racing cars, on the clothes and crash helmets* of the drivers as well as on the side of the racing circuit.

One Grand Prix racing team has received so much money from a cigarette company that it has painted the team cars in the colours of a famous cigarette packet.

Some teams have tried to race without sponsors. The Ferrari racing team, for example, raced for many years without large stickers on its cars. But even this team found that, in the end, it could not pay the bills without the help of sponsors.

4
Watching a race

The next time a Grand Prix race — or any motor race — takes place near your home, go along and see what happens there.

The drivers and their cars

If you want to enjoy the race, you should first of all find out who is going to race. You will probably know the famous drivers who are going to take part, but you will probably find it difficult to see who the drivers are when they shoot past you during the race. The best thing is to find out the colours of their cars, the colour of their helmets and, of course, the car numbers. If, before the race, you go to the place behind the pits called the paddock, you can see the drivers and their mechanics making last-minute changes to their cars. Most Grand Prix drivers have their names on the front of their clothes, or on their helmet, or even on their car.

If you can, look carefully at the cars themselves. Notice the large tyres at the back and the smaller ones at the front. Try to find out if the tyres are for racing in wet or dry weather. Notice the wings at the front and back of the car. These pieces of metal do not help the car to fly. In fact they do something quite different. When the car travels round the circuit, the air pushes down on to these wings and the wheels press* more firmly on to the road. This helps the car to go more safely round the bends and to go even faster along the straight parts of the circuit.

The racing circuit

When you have found out who is driving which car, you need to look for a place where you can watch the race. Some people think that watching a race can be very boring. It can be boring if you stand near a part of the circuit where the cars drive past very quickly. But if you stand near a bend, you can see the cars coming towards you, going slowly to get round the bend and then driving away as fast as possible. You will probably see the faster drivers passing the slower ones on a bend and, if you have a camera, you can take good photos of the cars.

If you have enough money you can pay to sit in the grandstand, a building at the side of the road, where you have a very good view of the start and finish, and also of the pits. You can also hear the loudspeakers* giving the latest news about the race.

Every racing circuit is different, so, if you have enough time, walk round the circuit and see the difficulties which the drivers will have in the race.

Brands Hatch

Le Mans

The practice and the start

Before each Grand Prix race the drivers must practise on the racing circuit. This practising can be almost as exciting as the real race, and many fans try to watch both. While he is practising, the driver can learn a lot about the circuit and, at the same time, decide whether the mechanics must make any changes to the engine, brakes or gears* of his car. When the mechanics have made all the necessary changes, the driver is then ready to drive as fast as possible around the circuit. The organisers measure the time which the driver needs to go once round the circuit, in other words to do one lap. These lap times are very important.

About twenty-six cars usually take part in a Grand Prix race. They cannot, of course, all start in a line across the track* because it is not wide enough. So the drivers form a sort of queue: two cars stand at the starting line, two more stand behind them, and so on.

How do you decide which drivers should be at the front of the queue? Years ago, chance used to decide: before the race each driver took a number from a bag. The driver with the lowest number could start at the front of the queue. Today the race organisers use a much better system. The driver who has made the fastest lap time in the practice driving for the race is the one who starts at the head of the queue.

It is easy to forget that, although the first and the last in this queue are hundreds of metres apart*, the difference in their lap times can be as little as one second!

The race

When all the cars are in their correct places at the start, and all the photographers, newspaper and television reporters have left the track, the starter* brings his flag down. The race is on*!

One of the most dangerous moments of any race is when the cars race towards the first bend. You can see the drivers fighting to get a good place in the race. Accidents can — and do — happen. The cars are very close together, the wheels can touch, and when they touch at one hundred kilometres an hour anything can happen.

It is on bends like these that the winner wins and the rest lose. All the cars in a race usually have the same engine power, and most of the drivers go at the same fast speed* along the straight parts of the circuit. The driver who can make his car go fastest through the bends is the one who will probably win the race.

After the cars have done several laps you can see that the drivers follow the same line when they go through the bends. Those who are watching, and those who are driving, soon notice the marks which the car tyres have made at each bend. This is the shortest but safest way through each of these bends.

It is, of course, impossible to see everything that happens during a race. But if you want to find out how well your favourite driver is doing, or how many laps the leader must do before the race finishes, you can go to the big notice-board which is usually near the grandstand.

The marshals can also tell the public — and the drivers — a lot about the race. These are men and women who

The chequered flag for the winner of a Grand Prix race

stand at the edge of the track and watch the race very carefully. When there is an accident, and several cars have stopped, the marshals show a yellow flag* to the drivers who are coming towards the scene* of the accident. The drivers must slow down and be ready to stop. When an ambulance* or fire engine comes on to the circuit — perhaps to go to a car which has crashed — the marshals wave a white flag. If the track is dangerous because there is oil on the road, the marshals must show a flag with red and yellow lines. When the track is clear, the marshals wave a green flag.

The favourite flag — for the leader of a race anyway — is the black and white flag which a marshal waves at the finish of a race. The crowds cheer and the winner drives slowly round the track and waves to everyone. Afterwards the driver and his team drink champagne, joke* with each other and talk to the reporters. For the winner, his team and his fans, it is the end of a great day.

For the other drivers it is a day when they almost won the race or when their car broke down or when they had a crash. . . .

5
Accident!

One of the first signs you see at a motor race meeting is
MOTOR RACING IS DANGEROUS. You see the sign everywhere, for the organisers do not want the spectators* to
forget that, wherever cars race, accidents can — and do —
happen. In fact motor racing is more dangerous than ever
because the cars go faster than ever.

We have already read that the drivers wear special
clothes which will not burn in an accident, and we already
know what the car builders must do to make their cars as
safe as possible. But what about the racing circuit? Race
organisers must not only tell spectators about the dangers
of motor racing, they must also make sure that spectators
can watch a race in as much safety as possible. They must,
for example, build special fences* around the circuit
which can catch any cars which leave the track at high
speed. Most accidents happen on bends, so here the
organisers must do all they can to save the lives of drivers
and spectators. They must, for example, cut down all
trees as well as knock down any buildings which are close
to the track. They must also, where possible, build
escape* roads at dangerous bends so that the driver can go
straight on if he finds that he is travelling too fast to go

round the bend.

When there is an accident, and people must receive help, the organisers must make sure that the ambulances can take them to a doctor or to a hospital immediately. At most Grand Prix races there is now a hospital on wheels where doctors can work just as well as in a normal hospital.

To show you how dangerous motor racing is we will now look at some serious* accidents where the drivers lived to tell the story.

Hospital on wheels at the Dutch Grand Prix 1967

Fire at Indianapolis

In May 1970, Denny Hulme was practising for the Indianapolis 500 mile race. While he was driving round the circuit at about 250 kilometres an hour he noticed that his car engine was shaking* a lot. But he did not notice that this shaking was slowly opening the top of one of his petrol tanks*.

Soon petrol started pouring out and the car caught fire. Denny saw the smoke and knew that in a few seconds the car was going to explode*. He knew also that there was not enough time to stop the car and get out. Jumping from the car was the only answer. When the fire reached the steering wheel, Denny climbed on to the car, ready to jump. He had to miss the wall round the circuit and the back wheels of his own car. He waited for the right moment and jumped.

To his surprise he was still in one piece when he got up from the ground. The car was a short distance away, against a post*, and fire and smoke were pouring from it.

Suddenly Denny saw that he was also on fire. Then a fire engine came towards him. It did not stop, but drove on to the car instead. This happened not because the firemen thought that the car was more important than the driver, but because they could not see that Denny Hulme was on fire! The petrol which Denny was using in his car was a very strong sort called methanol, and when methanol burns you cannot see the flames*.

Denny, his whole body now in flames, had to run to the firemen and ask them to put his fire out. He had some very bad burns, but four weeks after this accident he started racing again.

Jackie and the nuns

The Spa racing circuit in Belgium is probably the fastest and most dangerous in the world. It is fourteen kilometres long and runs through a forest*. Because it is such a long track you sometimes find that rain is falling at one end, but the other end of the circuit is dry.

In 1966 the Belgian Grand Prix was held there and many famous drivers took part. The start of the race was dry, but at the other end of the circuit it suddenly started raining. The race leaders drove into the sudden rain on a long right-hand bend. Eight drivers could not keep their cars on the wet track and left it. Jackie Stewart was one of them. He skidded off the track at 240 kilometres an hour, went through a couple of walls and then hit part of a house. He broke a few bones*, but his injuries were not really serious for such a bad crash. But the petrol tanks were broken and the cockpit* of the car was full of petrol. Jackie could not get out of his car because the crash twisted* the steering-wheel. The petrol was going into his clothes and burning his skin*.

Two other drivers came to free Jackie but could not do so with their hands alone. They found a spectator with a car who had some tools*. With one of them they were able to take off the steering-wheel. After half an hour Stewart was out of the car. No ambulance came. A helicopter appeared, but it was not for Jackie: the people inside were only taking a film of the race.

The drivers took off Jackie's clothes and went to look for help. Jackie, who was now almost unconscious*, thought he could see three nuns (women of the church)

Jackie Stewart

coming towards him. When they were close to him they started dressing him. Even now, after all these years, Jackie is still not sure whether these nuns were real or whether they were just a part of a dream which he had while he was lying on the grass.

In the end an ambulance arrived. The ambulance was, in fact, an old bus and Jackie had to lie on the floor on his way to hospital.

Crash in the Andes

High up in the Andes mountains in Argentina, the drivers who were taking part in the World Cup London to Mexico Rally* of 1970 were having a difficult time. The cars were on a special part of the rally where they had to drive nearly 900 kilometres in eight hours. The roads were terrible: narrow and very dusty.

Andrew Cowan, Brian Coyle and Laco Ossio were taking part in the rally in a Triumph car. Another rally car was in front of them, with Jean Denton at the wheel. She was driving very carefully through the mountains and, like all the other cars, was throwing up a lot of dust with the car wheels.

Andrew Cowan, the Triumph driver, could not pass the other car because the road was too narrow. He stayed behind, but could only just see the road because of the dust. The sun was coming up and Andrew was driving along at 130 kilometres an hour. He turned the wheel to follow the clouds of dust round a bend. But there was no bend. The Triumph went over the edge of the road, turned upside down and fell about twenty metres.

It was soon after this when Jean Denton, in the car in front, noticed that the Triumph was no longer behind. Should she try to find out why it was no longer following? It was very difficult to turn back. Perhaps the car was still there, but the dust was getting thicker. Perhaps the car had a flat tyre and the driver was changing the wheel. Jean decided that the only thing to do was to continue driving. She was, after all in a rally, and she wanted to win.

All three people in the Triumph were very badly hurt. The crash had knocked out* two of them, but Cowan was able to get out of the car and climb very slowly to the road. A lot of reporters and cameramen were following the rally cars and one of them saw Andrew Cowan on the side of the road. A car took all three to the nearest hospital where doctors decided that their injuries* were not too bad. But Cowan's neck was still hurting him a lot. A plane arrived to take them to a British hospital in Buenos Aires, but the weather was so bad that the plane could not leave for a week. When the three arrived at last in Buenos Aires, the doctors there found that Cowan's neck* was broken. They could not understand why he was not dead or why he could still move all the parts of his body.

Andrew Cowan, Jackie Stewart and Denny Hulme had good luck and they all lived to tell the story of their accident. But other drivers — many other drivers — have died. Some died immediately after their accident, others after many weeks or even months of pain. Motor racing brings fun to a lot of people, but it also brings a lot of unhappiness to others.

The old way of starting the Le Mans Grand Prix

6
Motor racing: something for everyone

We are now going to look at different sorts of motor racing. Some of these are as popular as Grand Prix racing, others even more popular.

Long-distance racing

Every year hundreds of thousands of motor racing fans go to Le Mans in France, to the old Grand Prix racing circuit there, to watch a race which lasts twenty-four hours. Among these fans are a lot of families who go for a weekend of fun. For around the circuit are lots of things to do and enjoy. There are shows, shops, markets, restaurants, cafés — and a very large fair.

The race starts in the afternoon. Until a few years ago, when the race started, the drivers had to run across the track to their cars and then drive off. But now the cars start the race in the normal way. By the end of the race the winner has driven nearly 5,000 kilometres. The circuit has a lot of bends, but also a straight part where cars have travelled as fast as 370 kilometres an hour. The cars which take part in the race are sports cars with big, powerful engines. Many famous car makers such as Bentley, Jaguar and Porsche have entered their cars in this race.

Every car has at least two drivers who take their turn at the wheel. It is a big test for them and for the mechanics, for the car must stop every few hours for petrol or fresh tyres, and the mechanics must change the wheels or fill the tanks as quickly as possible.

The race is also, in a way, a test for many of the spectators who stay awake all night to follow the race. Some of them just cannot keep their eyes open, and fall asleep. Others lose interest in the race when night falls, for then they can no longer see the cars, only the head-lights* which flash past.

Twenty-four hour races first started in the USA, and many people still watch them there. But the most famous long-distance race there is the Indianapolis 500. The race takes place on the Indianapolis Speedway which is two and a half miles long. As you can see from the picture, the circuit is very different from a Grand Prix one. The race is 500 miles long and the winner receives the largest money prize in motor racing. It is one of the fastest races in the world and it used to be the most dangerous. In 1973 there was a very serious accident during the race, so the organisers changed the rules to make the cars safer.

Rallying

You do not have to be rich to take part in a rally. Anyone who has a car, or who knows someone who has a car, can become a member of a rally club and enjoy a Sunday afternoon rally.

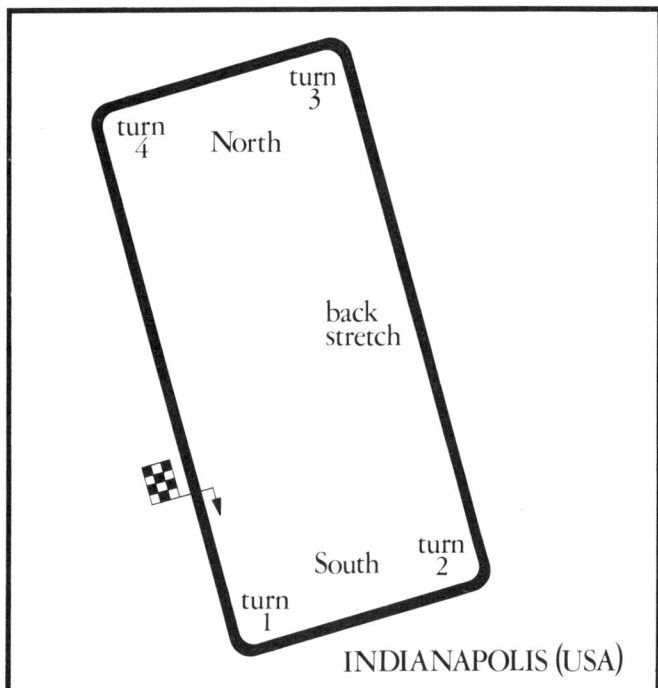

A rally is not the same as a race. The cars do not all start together, but leave the starting-line one at a time. They have to follow a route* and, on the way, they must report at checkpoints — places where the organisers write down the time of the car's arrival. If it arrives too early or too late the driver receives penalty* points. The rally winner is the driver who reports at all the checkpoints, follows the route correctly and arrives at the finish with the smallest number of penalty points.

A rally car

In Britain the cars which take part in a rally must not go faster than an average* of 30 miles per hour on normal roads or 50 miles per hour on motorways*. If the cars drive on private roads (which are not open to the public) they must keep to the average speed which the organisers have fixed.

A rally team has a driver and a navigator. The navigator sits next to the driver, looks carefully at the route instructions and the road map in front of him, and tells the driver where he must go. So even if you have not got a car — or cannot drive — you can still be a navigator in a rally team.

You have probably heard of the Monte Carlo Rally or the East African Safari Rally. There are many more rules for these than for the local* rallies, but the organisation of them is much the same. The route they follow is longer and much more difficult. The cars often drive through mountains, snow, ice or sand. The private roads which they use are either racing circuits or forest roads made of earth and rocks.

The longest rally took place in 1970 at the time of the World Cup football final* in Mexico. The cars started in London, drove across Europe to Bulgaria and Yugoslavia, then across to Portugal. From there the cars went by boat to Brazil. The route then went through Argentina, Peru and Chile and ended in Mexico City. It is not really surprising that less than one quarter of those cars which started the race were able to reach Mexico.

'Do it yourself' racing

If you want to race, but think that a Sunday rally is not very exciting, you can always go and climb a hill — in a car! For there are many sorts of racing which do not take place on racing circuits or public roads. You do not need to spend a lot of money on a fast, powerful car for these races.

If, for example, you want to take part in trials, you can buy a trials car for less than a thousand pounds. With the car you must climb hills where there are often rocks, old trees and even streams. If you stop on the way up, or leave the course, you lose points. You can go as slowly or as fast as you like. Every car has a passenger who jumps up and down on the seat to make the car go forwards on the difficult parts of the course.

In autocross, another similar sport, speed *is* important.

For autocross the circuit is in a field. The race is short, but exciting, because the driver must try to control his car in the mud* or on the grass as he goes round the circuit.

Rallycross is a very new motor sport. In the 1960s the makers of sports programmes on British television wanted to show more motor racing, like trials or auto-cross. So they invented* a race which is like both a rally and an autocross race. The cars — usually Minis — must not only drive along normal public roads but also over a special track which goes through a forest or fields.

Hillclimbing is the oldest sort of racing which takes place off a normal circuit. It first started in Britain when the British government stopped races on public roads. The course which the cars follow is usually about one kilo-metre long and has many bends. There are important international hill-climbing races where the course is much longer.

Race — in a straight line!

If you want to drive as fast as you can, but do not want to drive round dangerous bends, you can always take part in drag-racing.

This sport began in the United States in the 1950s and is now becoming popular in Europe. Dragsters are very strange-looking machines. They stand on the starting-line, one at a time. When the light changes to green they shoot off like a bullet from a gun. Smoke pours from the tyres and fire shoots out from the exhaust pipe*.

A dragster

The cars only race for a quarter of a mile, (just over half a kilometre), but in that short distance they can reach four hundred kilometres an hour. When they reach the finishing-line they are travelling so fast that the drivers must use a parachute* to stop the car.

Whether you are a Grand Prix driver, a hill-climber, a go-karter, a dragster, or just a race spectator, motor-racing offers fun, interest and excitement*.

Exercises

Chapter 1

1 How did the first car-builders check their cars?
2 Why did the governments in Europe stop motor racing on public roads?
3 What happens today to a Grand Prix driver who wins a lot of races?
4 What is a formula?
5 Why is the shape of a racing car important?

Chapter 2

1 How old was James Hunt when he decided he wanted to be a racing driver? What was he doing?
2 Why was Lord Hesketh important in the life of James Hunt?
3 Why did James leave the Hesketh team?
4 What do you think was the most important thing which helped James to become world champion? Explain why you think so.
5 What one thing was most important in helping James in the Japanese Grand Prix?

Chapter 3

1 What do the mechanics do before a race? What else happens in the pits?
2 Who often uses a stop-watch, and why?
3 Why is a racing car so expensive? How do racing teams get the money they need?
4 Why do you think cigarette companies can no longer show their names on television?
5 Do you think spectators remember the names on the racing car stickers whenever they go shopping for tyres or cigarettes?

Chapter 4

1 How can you find out who the drivers are when you are watching the race?
2 What should you look for when you look at the cars before the race?
3 What do you think is the best place to watch the race from? Why?
4 How does a race start? What has happened before it starts?
5 How can you find out what is happening during the ·race?

Chapter 5

1 List the things that are done to try to make racing as safe as possible.
2 Why did the firemen drive past Denny Hulme? What

did he have to do?
3 Describe Jackie Stewart's accident.
4 Which is the most dangerous racing circuit in the world?
5 What did Jean Denton do when she noticed the Triumph was no longer behind her car?

Chapter 6

1 How far does the winner of the Le Mans 24 – hour race usually drive?
2 What must a driver do to win a rally?
3 Why do you think so few cars reached the finish of the London – Mexico rally in 1970?
4 Name three sorts of racing you can do without a fast, powerful car?
5 What do you think is most important if you want to win a dragster race?

Language

1 Find the words in Chapter 1 which mean the same as:
   people who were watching
   a road only for motor racing
   the place where the road bends
   vintage
   what you must or must not do
   things which you use to put out fires

2 Find the words which are missing:
   Motor racing is one _____ the most dangerous sports.
   _____ must always remember that _____ cars race, acci-

dents can, _____ do, happen. Racing drivers must _____
special clothes which do _____ burn in an accident _____
car builders must make _____ cars as safe as _____. The
race organisers must _____ extra fences, cut down _____
which are close to _____ track and build escape _____ at
dangerous bends.

Look on page 56 for the answers.

3 Put the verbs into the past tense:
The first car with a petrol engine (is) built in 1885. The
first important motor race (takes) place ten years later.
Not many cars (finish) the race. Some (break down)
and some (crash). The races (become) faster and faster
and the people who (watch) (not understand) that fast
cars (are) such a danger to them.

Look on page 56 for the answers.

Writing

1 You have just seen a motor race for the first time.
Write a letter to a friend and tell him / her what you did
and what you saw.
Here are some notes to help you:
a *Before the race*
The scene in the paddock.
Describe the drivers and their cars.
b *The start of the race*
The scene at the starting line.
What can happen at the first bend?

c *During the race*

Where did you stand? Why? Did the marshals use their flags?

d *The finish*

What did the winner/the crowd/the reporters do?

2 Make a list of all the things which people do to make motor racing as safe as possible. Can you think of anything else which could be done?

3 Look again at the story of the crash in the Andes. You are Jean Denton. You have just finished a very difficult part of the rally — the part through the Andes. You are talking to a newspaper reporter. Tell him about:

a The difficult road.

b Andrew Cowan who was following you but suddenly disappeared. (What did you think when you no longer saw him behind you? Why didn't you go back?)

4 Do you think motor racing is a good thing or a bad thing? Why?

5 Which would you rather watch — a Grand Prix race or one of the various forms of rallying? Why?

Answers to Language exercise 2

Motor racing is one **of** the most dangerous sports. **Spectators** must always remember that **wherever** cars race, accidents can, **and** do, happen. Racing drivers must **wear** special clothes which do **not** burn in an accident **and** car builders must make **their** cars as safe as **possible**. The race organisers must **build** extra fences, cut down **trees** which are close to **the** track and build escape **roads** at dangerous bends.

Answers to Language exercise 3

The first car with a petrol engine **was** built in 1885. The first important race **took** place ten years later. Not many cars **finished** the race. Some **broke down** and some **crashed**. The races **became** faster and faster and the people who **watched/were watching did not understand** that fast cars **were** such a danger to them.

Glossary

accept   Take something that is offered to you.

accident   An accident happens when one car hits another car by mistake.

after   See *look after*.

ambulance   A special van (or car) which takes sick people to hospital.

amount (of petrol)   The number of litres.

apart   The cars are far apart — there is a large distance between them.

average   Some people earn £60, others earn £40. The average pay is £50.

bone   The hard parts inside your body.

bowler hat   A round black hat which many businessmen in London still wear.

brakes   When you want to stop your car, you use the brakes.

broke down   The car broke down — there was something wrong with it. It would not go.

career   He wants to make a career in motor racing — he wants to spend his life motor racing.

(to) catch fire   To start burning.

champagne   A famous French wine.

champion A driver becomes world champion when he is the best driver of all.

(to) check To look at something carefully, to see that it is OK.

cockpit Where the racing-driver (or the pilot of a plane) sits.

company A group of businessmen who buy and sell things. Industrial companies buy and sell things made by machines. Petrol companies buy and sell petrol.

couple Two.

crashed When two cars drove into each other they crashed.

cylinder Part of a car engine.

death When you stop living.

dozen Twelve. Half a dozen = six.

during At the same time as, while.

(to) enter Here, to enter a car. He decided to enter his car in the race — he decided to drive his car in the race.

escape road A road on which the driver can get away from the other cars.

excitement When you are very happy, or very interested in something you feel excitement.

exhaust pipe The smoke from a car engine goes into the air through an exhaust pipe.

explode He put too much air in the tyre, and it exploded — it went up in the air and broke into pieces.

extinguisher A bottle of water or other things which you use to put out fires.

(to) fall behind He fell behind in the race — he drove more and more slowly.

fan   She is fan of the Rolling Stones and has bought all their records. She likes them very much.

fence   A type of wall made of wood or metal.

final   The final is the last game of many.

flag   Piece of cloth which shows your club, country, town and so on. It is put on a stick and waved.

fire   See *catch fire*.

flames   The red and yellow parts of a fire.

(to) flash   When a photographer takes a photo he sometimes flashes a light to make the photo clearer.

forest   A group of many trees.

(the) future   The time after now.

gear   The part of the car which makes the engine turn more slowly or more quickly.

gloves   You wear gloves to keep your hands warm.

headlights   The big lights on the front of a car.

helicopter

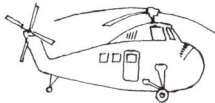

helmet   A strong hat which racing drivers wear.

injuries   Where you are hurt.

(to) invent   To find or make for the first time.

(to) joke   To tell funny stories.

lawn mower   A machine which cuts grass.

local   The local shops are the ones which you find near your home.

(to) look after   To keep something in good order — clean and working well.

lord   A title (a word which goes before your name). It

means you are important. There are kings, queens, lords — and the rest of us!

loudspeaker A thing which makes sounds louder, so many people can hear someone talking or playing music.

luck A good chance.

mechanic A man who works with machines. A hobby mechanic does this for fun and is not paid.

motorway A road where cars can go fast and pass each other easily.

mud A mixture of water and earth.

neck Your neck is between your head and your shoulders.

newcomer He is a newcomer to racing means he has just started racing.

on The race is on — the race has started.

operation When doctors cut your body, to make it better.

organiser Someone who makes plans for a race and who sees that all goes well during a race.

out See *knocked out*.

parachute He jumped out of the plane and fell slowly to earth; his parachute stopped him falling too fast.

penalty With so many penalty points, he lost the race — with so many points against him.. . .

perfume Special water which has a nice smell. Ladies put it on their faces.

pipe See *exhaust pipe*.

points In the world championship of drivers, the winner of a Grand Prix gets 9 points. The driver who comes second gets 6 points.

popular He is very popular — people like him very much.

position Place (in the race).

post A piece of wood; one end is in the ground.

(to) press To push.

prize He was first in the race and won a prize of £10,000!

pump You need a pump to put air into your tyre or to put petrol into your car.

recent A recent race is a race which happened not long ago.

replace The car is old; I must replace it with (get) a new one.

route Way. All the cars must follow the same route in a race.

rubber The tyres of a car are made of rubber.

rule Rules tell you what you must and must not do.

rally A sort of race, usually in ordinary cars.

scene The place where something (e.g. an accident) has happened.

secondhand Not new: when you buy a secondhand car, you buy a car from the person who first bought it.

serious A serious accident: an accident where people are badly hurt.

shake When you meet someone for the first time, you usually shake their hand.
The engine was shaking means the engine was moving up and down very quickly.

share Part of something.

similar Almost the same.

(to) skid When there is ice on the road, a car can easily skid when it is going too fast. It moves to the side.

skin The outside of your body.

solid A solid tyre has no air inside it and is very hard.

spare If a tyre on your car goes flat you must use the spare tyre — an extra tyre you can use if you need it.

speed The car is travelling at high speed. It is going very fast.

squash A ball game played inside, not outdoors. It is like tennis but the players use the walls of the court.

starter Here: the marshal who starts the race.

steam When water gets very hot, you can see steam coming off it. Water turns to steam when it is heated.

steering-wheel The driver of a car sits at the steering-wheel, which turns the wheels.

sticker A notice which you can stick anywhere.

stop-watch A special watch which you use to measure time during a race.

successful He passed his driving test — he was successful in the test.

(to) take part He wants to join in the race, but cannot because he has no car. He cannot take part.

tank The part of the car where you keep the petrol.

tennis Game played outdoors with racket and ball.

tent You sleep in a tent when you go camping.

tools Things you use to repair the car.

top A top driver is one who has come first in a lot of races.

track The road which the racing cars race.

(to) twist The crash twisted the steering-wheel. It turned it into a different shape.

unconscious The man knocked him out and he lay

unconscious on the floor. He did not see or hear anything. You are usually only unconscious for a few
minutes.

wages Money you get for your work.

windscreen The window at the front of a car.

yacht A boat with sails. It usually belongs to a rich man.